First World War
and Army of Occupation
War Diary
France, Belgium and Germany

42 DIVISION
125 Infantry Brigade,
Brigade Trench Mortar Battery
1 July 1917 - 31 December 1918

WO95/2655/4

The Naval & Military Press Ltd
www.nmarchive.com
Published in association with The National Archives

Published by

The Naval & Military Press Ltd

Unit 10 Ridgewood Industrial Park,

Uckfield, East Sussex,

TN22 5QE England

Tel: +44 (0) 1825 749494

www.naval-military-press.com

www.nmarchive.com

This diary has been reprinted in facsimile from the original. Any imperfections are inevitably reproduced and the quality may fall short of modern type and cartographic standards.

© **Crown Copyright**
Images reproduced by permission of The National Archives, London, England, 2015.

Contents

Document type	Place/Title	Date From	Date To
Heading	WO95/2655/4 125 Bde TM Batty 42 Div Jul 1917-Dec 1918		
Heading	42nd Division 125th Infy Bde Lt. Trench Mortar Batts Jly 1917-Dec 1918		
Heading	War Diary Of 125 Light Trench Mortar Battery July 1st 31st 1917 Vol. No. 3		
War Diary	Ytres	01/07/1917	06/07/1917
War Diary	Comiecourt	07/07/1917	31/07/1917
Heading	War Diary 125th Trench Mortar (Light) Battery August 1917 Vol No. 5		
War Diary	Comiecourt	01/08/1917	20/08/1917
War Diary	Bavincourt	21/08/1917	21/08/1917
War Diary	St Feans Ber Bigen	22/08/1917	29/08/1917
War Diary	Ypres	30/08/1917	31/08/1917
Heading	125th Light Trench Mortar Battery War Diary August 31st-September 30th 1917 Vol VI		
War Diary	St. Jan-Ter Biezen	30/08/1917	30/08/1917
War Diary	Ypres	31/08/1917	19/09/1917
War Diary	St. Jan-Ter-Biezen	21/09/1917	22/09/1917
War Diary	Arneke	23/09/1917	23/09/1917
War Diary	Esquelbecq	24/09/1917	24/09/1917
War Diary	Ghyvelde	25/09/1917	25/09/1917
War Diary	Coxide. Bains	27/09/1917	30/09/1917
Operation(al) Order(s)	125th Brigade Operation Order No. 34		
Map	H.3		
Miscellaneous	Message Form.		
Operation(al) Order(s)	125th Brigade Operation Order Number 35	04/09/1917	04/09/1917
Miscellaneous	Programme		
Operation(al) Order(s)	125th Brigade Operation Order Number 36	07/09/1917	07/09/1917
Operation(al) Order(s)	125th Brigade Operation Order Number 37	13/09/1917	13/09/1917
Operation(al) Order(s)	125th Brigade Operation Order Number 38	16/09/1917	16/09/1917
Miscellaneous	Relief Table To Accompany 125th Brigade Operation Order Number 38		
Operation(al) Order(s)	125th Brigade Operation Order No. 39	18/09/1917	18/09/1917
Operation(al) Order(s)	125th Brigade Operation Order No. 40	20/09/1917	20/09/1917
Operation(al) Order(s)	Addendum Number 1 To 125th Brigade O.O. No. 40	21/09/1917	21/09/1917
Operation(al) Order(s)	125th, Brigade Warning Order No. 41	24/09/1917	24/09/1917
War Diary	125th Brigade Order Number 42	25/09/1917	25/09/1917
War Diary	War Diary Of 125th Lt. Trench Mortar Battery Oct 1st-31st 1917 Vol VI		
War Diary	Coxyde-Bains	01/10/1917	02/10/1917
War Diary	Nieuport	05/10/1917	31/10/1917
Heading	War Diary of 125 Light Trench Mortar Battery Nov. 1st To 30th 1917 Vol No. 7		
War Diary	Coxide Canadacamp	02/10/1917	07/10/1917
War Diary	Nieuport	07/10/1917	08/10/1917
War Diary	Nieuport	07/10/1917	17/10/1917
War Diary	Coxyde	19/10/1917	20/10/1917
War Diary	Wormhoudt	21/10/1917	30/10/1917

Heading	Of 125 Light Trench Mortar Battery From 1 Dec 1917 to 31st Dec 1917		
War Diary	Le Preol	01/12/1917	01/12/1917
War Diary	Intheline	04/12/1917	08/12/1917
War Diary	Bethune	10/12/1917	22/12/1917
War Diary	Intheline	22/12/1917	29/12/1917
Heading	Of 125 Light Trench Mortar Battery From 1st Jan. 1918 To 31st Jan 1918		
War Diary	Festubert S 25d 5.4	01/01/1918	01/01/1918
War Diary	Givenchy A 9 a 9.1	05/01/1918	05/01/1918
War Diary	Prveure St. Pry A 21d 8.8	16/01/1918	16/01/1918
War Diary	Locon.	17/01/1918	17/01/1918
War Diary	Preveure St Pry A 21d 8.8	17/01/1918	17/01/1918
War Diary	Festubert S 25d 5.4	19/01/1918	19/01/1918
War Diary	Beuvry F14d 7.0	28/01/1918	29/01/1918
Heading	Of 125 Light Trench Mortar Battery From 1st February 1918 To 28th February 1918		
War Diary	Le Preol F10d5.3	01/02/1918	15/02/1918
War Diary	Drouvin K4 C 5.7	21/02/1918	24/02/1918
Heading	42nd Division 125th Infantry Brigade 125th Light Trench Mortar Battery March 1918		
Heading	125 Light Trench Mortar Battery From 1st March 1918 To 31st March 1918 Vol. 14		
War Diary	Drouvin K4 C 5.7 (Bethune Combd. Sheet)	01/03/1918	23/03/1918
War Diary	Adinfer Wood F2 b 9.9 (Sheet 57d 1/40,000)	23/03/1918	24/03/1918
War Diary	Gomiecourt (Sheet Lens N 1/100000 5 J. 5.8)	24/03/1918	24/03/1918
War Diary	Logeast Wood F30 C 7.5 (Sheet 57d 1/40,000)	25/03/1918	25/03/1918
War Diary	Adinfer Wood F2 B9.9	26/03/1918	26/03/1918
War Diary	Bienvilliers E 1 C 5.5 (Sheet 57d 1/40,000	27/03/1918	27/03/1918
War Diary	Essarts E. 24 b 7.2	30/04/1918	30/04/1918
Heading	125th Inf. Bde. 42nd Div. 125th Light Trench Mortar Battery. April 1918		
Heading	Volume No. 18 125 Light Trench Mortar Battery From 1st April 1918 to 30th April 1918		
War Diary	Commecourt Essarts	01/04/1918	08/04/1918
War Diary	Vauchelle 133 C	13/04/1918	15/04/1918
War Diary	Warnimont Wood	17/04/1918	20/04/1918
War Diary	Gommecourt K4 b30.35	29/04/1918	29/04/1918
Heading	War Diary of 125 Light Trench Mortar Battery from 1st May 1918 to 31st May 1918		
Miscellaneous	125 Bde. Ref A.L. 183 d/d 2/6/18	02/06/1918	02/06/1918
War Diary	Bayencourt J. 10 b 40.99 Sheet 57 D.N.E	01/05/1918	03/05/1918
War Diary	Gommecourt E 28d Central	06/05/1918	06/05/1918
War Diary	Couin Wood J 2 C (Sheet 5of D.N.E.)	29/05/1918	29/05/1918
Heading	125 Light Trench Mortar Battery from 1st June 1918 to 30th June 1918 Volume No. 17		
War Diary	Couin Woods J2c (Sheet 57d 1/40000)	01/06/1918	07/06/1918
War Diary	St. Leler Les Authie I12 C 6.6	13/06/1918	13/06/1918
War Diary	Bus. Woods. J 20 c 9.7	14/06/1918	14/06/1918
War Diary	Hebuterne	30/06/1918	30/06/1918
Heading	125 Light Trench Mortar Battery from 1st July 1918 to 31st July 1918 Volume No. 18		
War Diary	Hebuterne K 9c 2.7	01/07/1918	02/07/1918
War Diary	Bus Woods J 20 c 9.7	03/07/1918	10/07/1918
War Diary	Colincamps	26/07/1918	26/07/1918
War Diary	Bus Woods J 20 c 9.7	31/07/1918	31/07/1918

Heading	125 Light Trench Mortar Battery From 1st August 1918 To 31st August 1918 Volume No. 19		
War Diary	Bus Woods (J20 c 9.7)	01/08/1918	03/08/1918
War Diary	Colincamps (J 24d 6.8)	15/08/1918	31/08/1918
Heading	125 Light Trench Mortar Battery from 1st Sept 1918 to 30th Sept 1918 Volume No. 20		
War Diary	La Barque	01/09/1918	03/09/1918
War Diary	Barastre	05/09/1918	05/09/1918
War Diary	Pys	22/09/1918	29/09/1918
Heading	War Diary Of 125 L.T. M.By From 1/10/18 To 31/10/18 Volume No 21		
War Diary	Havrincourt Wood	01/10/1918	24/10/1918
War Diary	Fontaine	31/10/1918	31/10/1918
Heading	War Diary Of 125 L.T. M. By From 1/11/18 To 30/11/18 Volume No. 22		
War Diary	Fontaine Aupire	01/11/1918	12/11/1918
War Diary	Hautmont	30/11/1918	30/11/1918
Heading	War Diary of 125 L.T. M. By from 1/12/18 to 31/12/18 Volume No. 23		
War Diary	Hautmont Sheet 51	30/11/1918	18/12/1918
War Diary	Charleroi	31/12/1918	31/12/1918

WO95/2655 – 4

125 Bde T M Batty – 42 Div

Jul 1917 – Dec 1918

42ND DIVISION
125TH INFY BDE

LT. TRENCH MORTAR BATTS

JLY 1917-DEC 1918

CONFIDENTIAL
WAR DIARY
OF
125 LIGHT TRENCH MORTAR BATTERY

JULY 1ST 31ST, 1917

VOL. NO. 3.

WAR DIARY
or
INTELLIGENCE SUMMARY

(Erase heading not required.)

Army Form C. 2118

of 135 M.G. Battery

Place	Date	Hour	Summary of Events and Information	Remarks and references to Appendices
YPRES	July 1st		Battery at P.20.6.2.1 (57c) Battery Training Approximate Strength 4 Off 340R.	735.
"	July 2nd		Battery at same place. Training carried on	735.
"	July 3rd		Battery at same place. S.O.R.O (2 from each Battalion in Brigade) attacked to Battery for 1 months course of instruction. Training of Battery & reinforcements carried on also this day 7 men 2 from 5. B. 2 Dorset, 2 2007 & 1 D.82. J were permanently attached to Bty.	735.
"	July 4th		Battery Training carried on as usual.	735.
"	July 5th		Battery carried on training as usual. Having received Bgde orders to move to GOMIECOURT. Preparation for same	735.
"	July 6th		Left YPRES at 6 a.m. to travel with 135 Bgde to GOMIECOURT where we arrived at 17.30. Our Camp situation being A.23. C.8.9. 57C No. m fell out on route march.	735.
GOMIECOURT	July 7th 1917		Bty Training carried on at same place. Bty in tents.	735.
"	July 8th		Bty Training carried on as per programme of week previous to Bte.	735.
"	July 9th		Bty Training carried on. 10//& 80R going to 8P.L.J for instruction in discipline & drill under Guards Instructors	735.

WAR DIARY
or
INTELLIGENCE SUMMARY

Army Form C. 2118

1/3 5 M.G. Battery

Place	Date	Hour	Summary of Events and Information	Remarks and references to Appendices
BONNECOURT	July 10th		Same as July 9th. Strength of Bty 4 Officers 47 OR.	935.
"	July 11th		Same as July 9th	935.
"	July 12th		Bty Training as per Programme	935.
"	July 13th		Bty Training as per Programme	935.
"	July 14th		Bty Training carried on as per Programme	935.
"	July 15th		" " " "	935.
"	July 16th		Signalling course for all Signallers in Bty	935.
"	July 17th		" " " "	935.
"	July 18		" " " "	935.
"	July 19th		Bty took part in Trench to Trench attack. 100 live rounds expended 4 Gun Team employed. Strength of Bty 4 Officers 46 OR's	935.
"	July 20th		Bty Training Shot. 3 days Bombing course under B.B.O	935.
"	July 21		Bty on Bombing course as before	935.
"	July 22		" " " "	935.

Army Form C. 2118

WAR DIARY
— or —
INTELLIGENCE SUMMARY
(Erase heading not required.)

of 125 Trench Battery

3.

Place	Date	Hour	Summary of Events and Information	Remarks and references to Appendices
COMIECOURT	July 23rd		Bty Training as per programme	9B2.
"	July 24th		Bty Training as per programme	9B2.
"	July 25th		" " " "	9B2.
"	July 26th		Inspection G.O.C. 125 Inf Bde Dress Full Marching order on own camp ground	9B2.
"	July 27th		Bty Training as per programme	9B2.
"	July 28th		" " " "	9B2.
"	July 29th		" " " "	9B2.
"	July 30th		" " " "	9B2.
"	July 31st		Bty Strength 4 Officers 95 O.R.	9B2.
			Weather during the month has on the whole been good but with occasional thunderstorms. There was slight sickness in the Battery, mostly minor ailments such as foot trouble, boils & septic sores.	

D B Slater
Capt
O/C 125 Trench Mortar Battery.

CONFIDENTIAL.

WAR DIARY

125th Trench Mortar (Light)
Battery

August 1916
—
Vol No: 5

Army Form C. 2118

WAR DIARY
or
INTELLIGENCE SUMMARY
(Erase heading not required.)

of 1/125 Trench Mortar Battery

Instructions regarding War Diaries and Intelligence Summaries are contained in F.S. Regs., Part II. and the Staff Manual respectively. Title Pages will be prepared in manuscript.

Place	Date	Hour	Summary of Events and Information	Remarks and references to Appendices
BOMIECOURT Aug	Aug 1st		Battery Training carried on in Camp. Map Ref. A.23.C.8.9. As stated in weekly Programme.	APC
"	Aug 2nd		Battery Training Carried on as above. A.23.C.8.9	APC
"	Aug 3rd		Battery Training Carried on as above. A.23.C.8.9	APC
"	Aug 4th		Battery Training Carried on as above. A.23.C.8.9	AM
"	Aug 5th		Battery Training Carried on as above. A.23.C.8.9	M.
"	Aug 6th		Battery Training Carried on as above. A.23.C.8.9	SR.
"	Aug 7th		Battery Training carried on as above. A.23.C.8.9. Battery Strength off EC.	AM.
"	Aug 8th		Battery Training Carried on as as per Weekly Training State	AM.

WAR DIARY
of 1/5 Trench Mortar Battery
INTELLIGENCE SUMMARY

Army Form C. 2118

(Erase heading not required.)

Place	Date	Hour	Summary of Events and Information	Remarks and references to Appendices
Romiecourt	Aug 9th		Hors. H.W. A.23.C.8.9. Capt Elchia H'quarters Batty Training carried on as per Weekly Training Stat-Command of Battery Programme. proceeded to 1st Corps School	AR.
"	" 10th		Battery Training carried on as per programme. A.23.C.8.9	AR.
"	" 11th		" " " " " A.23.C.8.9	AR.
"	" 12th		" " " " " A.23.C.8.9	AR.
"	" 13th		" " " " " A.23.C.8.9	AR.
"	" 14th		Battery Strength " of 4 34 Tth " A.23.C.8.9	AR.
"	" 15th		" " " " " A.23.C.8.9	AR.
"	" 16th		" " " " " A.23.C.8.9	AR.
"	" 17th		" " " " " A.23.C.8.9	AR.
"	" 18th		" " " " " A.23.C.8.9	AR.
"	" 19th		" " " " " A.23.C.8.9	AR.

WAR DIARY
or 125 Trench Mortar Battery
INTELLIGENCE SUMMARY

(Erase heading not required.)

Army Form C. 2118

Instructions regarding War Diaries and Intelligence Summaries are contained in F.S. Regs., Part II. and the Staff Manual respectively. Title Pages will be prepared in manuscript.

Place	Date	Hour	Summary of Events and Information	Remarks and references to Appendices
CONNECOURT	Aug. 20th		Left Connecourt for Bouzincourt arrived Bouzincourt 3.30. (M.13.B.6.2.d.)	M.
BOUZINCOURT	" 21st		Battery utilized cleaning up camp which was found to be in a very unsatisfactory (M.13.B.2.d) condition	M.
St. Jean-ter-Biezen	" 22nd		Left Bouzincourt proceeding to Alvert Station where we entrained for Godewaersvelde Stur 27	M.
"	" 23rd		Battery Training carried on as usual. Stur 27. L12 d 3 where we detrained marching a distance of 5 miles to St Jean (L1 D43)	M.
"	" 24th		" " " " " " L12 d 3	M.
"	" 25th		" " " " " " L12 d 3	M.
"	" 26th		" " " " " " L12 d 3	M.
"	" 27th		" " " " " "	M.
"	" 28th		" " " " " "	M.
"	" 29th		Left L12 d3 M Poperinghe Station where we entrained for M.Pres.. detraining at the Asylum M12 D28. Stw.28. where we marched to H18 c.67. Stw.28	M.
YPRES	" 30th		Left Ypres for Mill. Cof. reconnoitre we relieved the 46 T.M.B. 67. H18 c.67 actually but in the line no guns were	M.
"	" 31st		Improvements of Shelters & Sheds carried on – during day when possible	M.

A. Walter Cooper Lieut.
OC. 125 T.M.B.

125th LIGHT TRENCH MORTAR BATTERY

WAR DIARY

AUGUST 31st – SEPTEMBER 30th 1917.

Vol. VI

Army Form C. 2118

WAR DIARY
of
INTELLIGENCE SUMMARY 125TH LIGHT TRENCH MORTAR BATTERY.

(Erase heading not required.)

Instructions regarding War Diaries and Intelligence Summaries are contained in F.S. Regs, Part II. and the Staff Manual respectively. Title Pages will be prepared in manuscript.

Place	Date	Hour	Map Reference	Summary of Events and Information	Remarks and references to Appendices
ST. JAN-TER BIEZEN	30.8.17	—	FRANCE SHEET 27. 1/40000	BATTERY HDQRS. STATIONED AT L.2.a.2.8.	APC
YPRES	3.8.17	8 P.M.	FRANCE SHEET 28. 1/40000	BATY. RECEIVED ORDERS TO MOVE TO YPRES AREA. BATY HDQRS TO BE AT CAMBRIDGE RD. I.5.A.3.5.	APC
	3.8.17	8.50 AM		BATY. MOVED BY MARCH ROUTE TO CAMP IN H.17.d. ARRIVING AT 5 P.M. NO MEN FELL OUT.	APC
"	1.9.17	6.30 P.M.	DO.	" — CAMBRIDGE RD. " 10.15 P.M.	APC
"				BTY. TOOK OVER FROM 46TH L.T.M.B. PORTION OF LINE N.E. OF YPRES. J.14.9.1. — D.19.d.0.5.	APC
	5.9.17	3.30 PM		2/LT. C.F. FRENCH WOUNDED BY RIFLE BULLET WHILE RECONN. LINE.	APC
	5.9.17	10 PM		6 GUNS TAKEN UP TO LOW FARM D.25.a.6.5. TO ASSIST ATTACK ON CONCRETE REDOUBTS AT BECK HOUSE, BORRY FARM, + IBERIAN D.19.L. D.25.L	APC
	5.9.17	11.15 PM		PARTY GOING UP WITH GUNS CAUGHT IN ENEMY BARRAGE D.25.a. 7 O.R.s WOUNDED. 2 O.R. SUFFERING FROM SHELL SHOCK. 3 GUN TEAMS BECAME CASUALTIES.	APC APC
	6.9.17	10.30 AM		2 GUNS PLACED IN POSITION	APC APC
	6.9.17	7.30 AM		100 ROUNDS FIRED IN SUPPORT OF ATTACK AS BARRAGE IN FRONT OF BORRY FARM.	
	6.9.17	6 PM	DO.	RECEIVED ORDERS TO WITHDRAW GUNS TO CAMBRIDGE RD. ON RELIEF BY 127TH L.T.M.B. 5 GUNS TAKEN BACK. [1 GUN DESTROYED BY SHELL FIRE]	APC
		10.30 PM		RELIEVED AT CAMBRIDGE RD. FROM ASYLUM H.12. d.8.7. MOVE BY TRAIN TO ST. LAWRENCE CAMP. G.11. CENT	APC
	10.9.17	10.30 PM		RECEIVED ORDERS TO TAKE OVER SAME LINE FROM 127 L.T.M.B.	APC
	11.9.17	6.45 PM		MOVED TO CAM BRIDGE RD. AND TOOK OVER SAME LINE FROM 127 L.T.M.B.	APC
	13.9.17	4 PM		2 O.R.s KILLED BY SHELL AT MILL COTT. I.4.L.9.5.85.	APC
	16.9.17	7.30 AM		RECEIVED ORDERS TO BE RELIEVED BY 1ST S.A. BRIGADE L.T.M.B.	APC
	"	4.30 PM		RELIEVED BY 1ST S.A. BDE L.T.M.B.	APC
		9 PM		MARCHED LEVEL CROSSING H.11.CENT AND ENTRAINED FOR ST. LAWRENCE CAMP. ARRIVING 2 AM.	APC
	17.9.17	8.30 AM	FRANCE SHEET 27. 1/40000	REINFORCEMENTS: 12 O.R.s ARRIVED FROM 125 INF. BDE.	APC
	18.9.17	9 PM		RECEIVED ORDERS TO MOVE TO SCHOOLS CAMP L.S.CENT	APC
	19.9.17	11.7 AM		STARTED BY MARCH ROUTE FOR SCHOOLS CAMP ARRIVING 1.30 PM.	APC

Army Form C. 2118

WAR DIARY
INTELLIGENCE SUMMARY
(Erase heading not required.)

of 125TH LIGHT TRENCH MORTAR BATTERY.

Place	Date	Hour	Map Reference	Summary of Events and Information	Remarks and references to Appendices
ST JAN-TER-BIEZEN	21.9.17	1.P.M.	FRANCE SHEET 27 1/40000	ORDERS RECEIVED TO ENTRAIN AT HOPOUTRE FOR ARNEKE.	
	21.9.17	6.55 P.M		ENTRAINED AT HOPOUTRE.	
	22.9.17	1.15 A.M		DETRAINED AT ARNEKE AND MOVED INTO BILLETS. BATY H.Q. ORS AT H.24.a.9.4.	
ARNEKE	23.9.17	2.0 P.M.	BELGIUM SHEET 11.	ORDERS RECEIVED TO ENTRAIN FOR GHYVELDE. MARCHING TO ESQUELBQ STATION.	
ESQUELBECQ	24.9.17	2.30 P.M	"	ENTRAINED FOR GHYVELDE, ARRIVING AT 5 P.M. BATY. H.Q. ORS AT D.16. CENT.	
GHYVELDE	25.9.17	7.0 A.M.	"	ORDERS RECEIVED TO MARCH TO ST. IDESBALD AREA. RELIEVE 199TH L.T.M.B.	
	25.9.17	1.45 P.M	"	STARTING BY MARCH ROUTE FOR ST IDESBALD AREA ARRIVING 5.15 P.M. BTY. H.Q. ORS AT COXIDE-BAINS W.5.d.95.95.	
	27.9.17	5.30 P.M	"	1 O.R. RETURNED FOR DUTY FROM HOSPITAL.	
COXIDE-BAINS	29.9.17	10.30 A.M	D.O.	LIEUT. A.A. DICKSON FROM 178TH L.T.M.B. REPORTED TO ASSUME COMMAND OF BATTERY.	
	29.9.17	5.15 P.M		REINF. 1 O.R. REPORTED FOR DUTY.	
	30.9.17	5.30 P.M		" 2 " " " "	

A.A. Dickson
Lieut 125 L.T.M.B.

SECRET.   Copy No. 22

125th BRIGADE OPERATION ORDER No.34.

Ref Map FREZENBERG $\frac{1}{10,000}$.

1.   The following Reliefs will take place on Night 4th/5th inst.

(a) RIGHT SUBSECTOR.

    5th Lan Fus less 2 Companies) will relieve 7th Lan Fus.
    2 Companies 6th Manchesters) in Front Line.

The Battalion Front will be held by 2 Companies 5th Lan Fus in the Line and 2 Companies 6th Manchesters in Support.

7th Lan Fus will be withdrawn into Right Support.

(b) LEFT SUBSECTOR.

    6th Lan Fus, 3 Companies.) will relieve 8th Lan Fus less
    2 Companies 6th Manchesters) 1 Company in Front Line.

The Battalion Front will be held by 1 Company 6th Lan Fus and 1 Company 8th Lan Fus in the Line and 2 Companies 6th Manchesters in Support.

    8th Lan Fus less 1 Company will be withdrawn into Left Support.

2.   Completion of relief to be reported to Brigade Headquarters.

3.   A C K N O W L E D G E.

                                                                     Captain,
                                                              Brigade Major,
                                                             125th BRIGADE.

Issued at 7.p.m.

Copies to:-

1.	5th Lan Fus.	13.	Signalling Officer.
2.	6th Lan Fus.	14.	B. T. O.
3.	7th Lan Fus.	15.	126th Brigade.
4.	8th Lan Fus.	16.	127th Brigade.
5.	125th M.G.Company.	17.	182 nd Brigade.
6.	125th T.M.Battery.	18.	42nd Division.
7.	427th Field Coy R.E.	19.	Right Sub Group Artillery.
8.	428th Field Coy R.E.	20.	Left Sub Group Artillery.
9.	429th Coy A.S.C.	21)	
10.	Brigade Major.	22)	F! !.!.!.B. War Diary.
11.	Staff Captain.	23.	F I L E.
12.	Rear Staff Captain.		

1:10 000.   H.3.

ENEMY TRENCHES
POSTS ○○○○
OUR POSITIONS
M.G. POSITIONS ▬▬▬

Scale. 1:10,000.

Message Form.

..........................Division.

Map reference or mark own position on Map at back.

I am at..

I am at..and am consolidating.

I am at..and have consolidated.

I need :—Ammunition.
　　　　Bombs.
　　　　Rifle Grenades.
　　　　Water.
　　　　Very lights.
　　　　Stokes shells.

Enemy forming up for counter-attack at...

I am in touch with....................on Right / Left at...

I am not in touch on Right / Left.

Am being shelled from...

I estimate my present strength at....................rifles.

Hostile { Battery / Machine Gun / Trench Mortar } active at...

Time　　a.m. (p.m.)　　　　Name................................
Date..................................　　　Platoon...........Company...........
Place................................　　　Battalion..............................

S E C R E T.   Copy No. 19

125th BRIGADE OPERATION ORDER NUMBER 35   4/9/17.

Map Reference FREZENBERG Edition 3   1/10,000

1. The 125th Brigade will attack and capture the Strong Points in the neighbourhood of BORRY FARM, BECK HOUSE and IBERIAN on 'Z' Day.
   The 61st Division is attacking GALLIPOLI on the same day and at the same time.

2. The 5th Lan Fus will attack BORRY with 2 Companies.
   The 6th Lan Fus will attack BECK with 1 Company and IBERIAN 2 Companies.

3. The Table of Artillery Barrage and Gas Bombardment is attached. Barrage Map will be issued later.

4. Instructions for R.E. for consolidation of the Objectives have been issued to all concerned, &c., in 125th BRIGADE INSTRUCTIONS NUMBER 1 dated 3rd inst.

5. Instructions for M.Gs have been issued to all concerned in 125th BRIGADE INSTRUCTIONS NUMBER 2 dated 4th inst.

6. Instructions for T.M.Battery have been issued to all concerned in 125th BRIGADE INSTRUCTIONS Number 3 dated 4th inst.

7. Dress for assaulting Companies:-
   Go over Kit without Entrenching Tools, Haversacks, Bombs or Flares. /each man will carry the following:-
   3 Sandbags.
   (1 Lewis Gun Drum (Lewis Gun Teams will carry the usual
   (number of Drums.
   1 Day's rations (In addition to the Iron Ration)
   1 Extra Water Bottle (Attached on Left Side)
   200 Rounds S.A.A.
   Waterproof Sheet.
   Bombers will carry 8 Bombs a man.
   Rifle Grenadiers, 6 Rifle Grenades each.
   (M.G.Company 1 Day's Rations (In addition to Iron Ration)
   (and an Extra Water Bottle.

8. Watches will be Synchronised by an Officer from Brigade Headquarters on 'Y' Day.

9. 'Z' Day and Zero Hour will be notified later.

10. A C K N O W L E D G E.

                                                                A.Lawrence
                                                                Captain,
                                                                Brigade Major,
Issued at......a.m. by Signals.   125th BRIGADE.
Copies to:-
1. 5th Lan Fus.   11. 42nd Division.
2. 6th Lan Fus.   12. Right Sub Group Artillery.
3. 7th Lan Fus.   13. Left Sub Group Artillery.
4. 8th Lan Fus.   14. Special Companies R.E.
5. 125th M.G.Company.   15. Brigade Major.
6. 125th T.M.Battery.   16. Staff Captain.
7. 126th M.G.Company.   17. Signalling Officer.
8. 127th M.G.Company.   18)
9. 126th Brgade.   19) War Diary.
10. 127nd Brigade.   20. F I L E.

PROGRAMME

'Z' Day. 2.30.a.m. (Projection of Gas on BORRY FARM, BECK HOUSE and
              (IBERIAN by Special Coys R.E.

4.30.a.m.   (Occasional Gas Shell by 4.5. Howitzers. Objectives on
to 6.30.a.m. (to be attacked, and on other Targets in the vicinity.

7.0.a.m.   (Bombardment of selected Targets by Flanking Corps
              (Artillery.

Zero - 15   (Intensive Bombardment of three Objectives with 6inch
to Zero.   (Howitzers.

Zero - 15   (Smoke Barrage on Line D 26 a 35.70. - BREMEN REDOUBT
for 1 Hour. (- D 20 a 5.5., from D 26 d 0.0. towards Brick Kiln
              (and Yard, and also to blot out BIT WORK and VAMPIR.

Zero.   (Creeping Barrage comes down in front of our Trenches
              (and lifts 100 yards every 5 minutes, eventually forming
              (protective barrage beyond Objectives.

Zero.   (6inch Howitzers lift to form a protective barrage
              (beyond the line on which the 18 pounder protective barr
              (age will eventually rest.

Zero.   (4.5. Howitzers. Bombardment of certain selected points
              (to close to objectives for 6inch Howitzers to shoot at.

Zero.   (Smoke Screen on and just beyond BORRY FARM, BECK HOUSE
              (and IBERIAN from MORTARS of Special Coys R.E.

War Diary

SECRET.   Copy No. 2

125th BRIGADE OPERATION ORDER NUMBER 36.   7/9/17.

Reference FREZENBERG Map 1/10,000

1. 125th Brigade will be relieved in the Left Sector of 42nd Divisional Front by 127th Brigade on Night 7th/8th September.

2. The 4 Companies 6th Manchester Regiment now attached to 6th Lan Fus will revert to their own Unit on completion of Relief.

3. 5th Lan Fus (Right Front)   ) Will be relieved by 5th
   2 Companies 6th Manchester Regt) Manchester Regt

   6th Lan Fus (Left Front)   )
   2 Companies 6th Manchester Regt   ) Will be relieved by 8th
   3 Companies 8th Lan Fus   ) Manchester Regt.

   7th Lan Fus will be relieved by 7th Manchester Regt.

   8th Lan Fus (Less 3 Companies) will be relieved by 6th Manchester)
                                                                Regt)

4. 2 Guides per Battalion Headquarters, 1 per Company H.Q., and 1 per Platoon will be found and rendezvous as under:-

   By 5th Lan Fus at MENIN GATE at 8.p.m.
   By 6th Lan Fus at Brigade H.Q. at 8.45.p.m.
   By 125th M.G.Company at Brigade H.Q. at 9.p.m.
   By 7th Lan Fus at MENIN GATE at 10.p.m.
   By 8th Lan Fus   ) Junction of 'G' Track and FREZENBERG
   for 6th Manchester H.Q.) Road at 10.15.p.m.
) Brigade H.Q. at 10.30.p.m.
   By 125th T.M.Battery at Brigade H.Q. at 11.p.m.

5. 125th M.G.Company will leave 2 Sections to be at the Disposal of G.O.C. 127th Brigade.

6. It is hoped that an Officer from each Battalion of 127th Brigade will come up in Advance. If not each Guide will be given a piece of Paper stating Right or Left Front, Right or Left Support and the Company and Platoon to which he belongs.

7. Great care is to be taken over the Relief and no Unit is to leave its Trench until Relieved.

8. One N.C.O. per Front Line Company will remain in for 24 Hours and then rejoin his Unit.

9. Should there be any Points of Tactical Importance held by Lewis Guns, and should the O.C. of the Relieving Battalion so desire, the Gun and Team will remain in for 24 Hours.

10. All Trench and Area Stores, Maps, Photographs, Sketches will be handed over on Relief and a receipt obtained.

(2)

11. 125th Brigade will take over the Camp vacated by the 127th Brigade in the BRANDHOEK Area.

12. The Brigade will be moved by Train and Bus from YPRES. Details will be issued later by the Staff Captain.

13. Rear Staff Captain is responsible for Guides meeting all Units at the Detraining and Debussing Points and Guiding them direct to their Camps.

14. Relief Complete to be reported at Brigade Headquarters at MILL COTT.

15. A C K N O W L E D G E.

A.T.Lawrence
Captain,
Brigade Major,
125th BRIGADE.

Issued at 2 am by SDR

Copies to:-
1. 5th Lan Fus.
2. 6th Lan Fus.
3. 7th Lan Fus.
4. 8th Lan Fus.
5. 125th M.G.Company.
6. 125th T.M.Battery.
7. 127th Brigade.
8. 42nd Division.
9. 429th Company A.S.C.
10. Rear Staff Captain.
11. B.T.O.
12. 182nd Brigade.
13. 126th Brigade.
14. Brigade Major.
15. Staff Captain.
16. Signalling Officer.
17) War Diary.
18)
19. F I L E.

SECRET.   Copy No. 20

125th BRIGADE OPERATION ORDER NUMBER 37.   13/9/17.

Reference PEIZENBERG $\frac{1}{10,000}$.

1. 125th Brigade will relieve 127th Brigade in the Left Sector of the Divisional Front on Night 14th/15th inst.

2. **RIGHT SUBSECTOR.**

   7th Lan Fus will relieve 5th Manchesters in Front Line.

   5th Lan Fus will relieve 7th Manchesters in Support.

   LEFT SUBSECTOR.

   8th Lan Fus will relieve 8th Manchesters in Front Line.

   6th Lan Fus will relieve 6th Manchesters in Support.

   Units will march in above order.

3. One Guide per Company Headquarters and One per Platoon will meet incoming Units at MILL COTT.

4. Train Arrangements will be issued by the Staff Captain later.

5. After Detraining, Units will march with 200 yards interval between Platoons.

6. 5, 6, and 7th Lan Fus will each send an Officer to be at 127th Brigade Headquarters by 10.a.m. to-morrow.
   All other Details of relief to be made by C.Os concerned.

7. 125th T.M.Battery will take over the same accommodation as they occupied before in CAMBRIDGE ROAD.
   The Guns may be sent up in Daylight.

8. 125th M.G.Company will relieve 127th M.G.Company under arrangements to be made by C.Os concerned.

9. All Tools, S.A.A., Rockets, Bombs, Maps and Photographs will be taken over on relief.

10. Relief complete to be wired to Brigade Headquarters in B.A.B.

11. A C K N O W L E D G E.

                                                                   Captain,
                                                                   Brigade Major,
                                                                   125th BRIGADE.

Issued at. 4.p.m.

Copies to:-
1. 5th Lan Fus.   12. 428th Field Coy R.E.
2. 6th Lan Fus.   13. 42nd Division.
3. 7th Lan Fus.   14. C.R.A. 42nd Division.
4. 8th Lan Fus   15. C.R.E. 42nd Division.
5. 125th M.G.Company.   16. 126th Brigade.
6. 125th T.M.Battery.   17. 127th Brigade.
7. Brigade Major.   18. 184th Brigade.
8. Staff Captain.   19. B. T. O.
9. Signals.   20) War Diary.
10. 429th Coy A.S.C.   21)
11. 427th Coy R.E.   22. F I L E.

SECRET.   Copy No........

125th BRIGADE OPERATION ORDER NUMBER 38.   16/9/17.

Map Reference. FREZENBERG. $\frac{1}{10,000}$

SHEET 28 N.E. $\frac{1}{20,000}$

1. 125th Brigade will be relieved in the Left Sector of the Divisional Front by the South African Brigade on the Night 17th/18th September as per attached Table.

2. On relief the Brigade Group will be concentrated in BRANDHOEK Number 2 Area. Battalions, Machine Gun Company and Trench Mortar Battery will train from Asylum.

3. Units will march with 200 yards interval between Platoons. All other Details of Relief to be arranged between C.Os concerned. Relief Complete to be reported by Wire.

4. All Air photographs, all $\frac{1}{10,000}$ FREZENBERG Maps, Message Maps (H.3) and Sun Prints will be handed over on Relief. All linen backed Maps will be kept.

5. Administrative Instructions will be issued by Staff Captain.

6. Rear Brigade Headquarters and Details will move to the New Area by Noon 17th inst and Rear Brigade Headquarters will open at H 7 a 2.2 at 1.p.m.

7. Brigade Headquarters will close at HILL COTT at 6.a.m. 18th inst and re-open at H 7 a 2.2.
   Command of Sector will pass to G.O.C. South African Brigade at this Hour.

8. ACKNOWLEDGE.

                                                        Captain,
                                                        Brigade Major,
                                                        125th BRIGADE.

Issued at 12.Noon through Signals.
Copies to :-

1. 5th Lan Fus.   14. Lt Clemes.
2. 6th   "   "   15. B. T. O.
3. 7th   "   "   16. 42nd Division.
4. 8th   "   "   17. 42nd Division "Q"
5. 125th M.G.Company.   18. A.D.M.S. 42nd Division.
6. 125th T.M.Battery.   19. No.2 Sub Group Artillery.
7. 427th Field Coy R.E.   20. No.3. "   "   "
8. 429th Coy A.S.C.   21. No.4. "   "   "
9. 1/1st E.L.Field Amb.   22. 126th Brigade.
10. Brigade Major.   23. 166th Brigade.
11. Staff Captain.   24. 27th Brigade.
12. Rear Staff Captain.   25. South African Brigade.
13. Signal Officer.

RELIEF TABLES TO ACCOMPANY 125th BRIGADE OPERATION ORDER NUMBER 38.

No.	(a) UNIT	(b) RELIEVED BY	(c) FROM	(d) TO.	(e) REMARKS.
1.	7th Lan Fus.	3rd S.A. Inf.	Right Front Headquarters WILDE WOOD.	G 11 c 6.6.	2 Guides for Battalion Headquarters, 1 per Company Headquarters and 2 per Platoon of 3 Companies in Front Line 8.p.m. 1 for Headquarters and 1 per Platoon of Reserve Company 9.p.m.
2.	8th Lan Fus.	4th S.A. Scottish.	Left Front Headquarters SQUARE FARM.	G 10 d 9.3.	d i t t o.
3.	5th Lan Fus.	1st S.A. Inf.	Right Support Headquarters I-11 b.4.10	G 11 c 4.4.	2 Guides per Battalion Headquarters, 1 per Company Headquarters and 1 per Platoon 9. p. m.
4.	6th Lan Fus.	2nd S.A. Inf.	Left Support Headquarters HILL COTT.	G 11 c 6.3.	d i t t o.
5.	125th M.G.Coy.	28th M.G.Coy.	Headquarters HILL COTT.	H 7 a 3.3.	Details to be arranged between C.Os concerned.
6.	125th T.M.Be tty.	S.A. Bde T.M.Betty.	Headquarters I 5 d 4.5.	G 11 c 4.8.	Guides at 8.p.m.
7.	427th Fd Coy.R.E.		RAMPARTS.	G 12 b 5.8.	On 17th inst under orders of C.R.E. 42nd Divn
8.	1/1st E.L. Fd Ambulance.			G 12 b 8.7.	Under orders of A. D. M. S. 42nd Division.

N.B. All Guides will rendezvous at the MENIN GATE at times stated in Column (c). Each will be provided with a paper stating the Unit and Platoon he belongs to and the Unit and Platoon for which he is to act as Guide. Owing to the Relieving Brigade coming up by train, complete Units may not be on the same train; Guides will therefore wait until their parties arrive although they may be later than is stated above.

SECRET. 125th BRIGADE OPERATION ORDER NO.39.

Copy No. 16.
19/9/17.

Ref: Sheets 27. N.E. & 28 N.W. 20,000.

1. The 125th Brigade Group will march from present Area to ST JAN - TER - BIEZEN Area on 19th inst as under :-

2. Route Switch Road N of POPERINGHE - road junction L 4 b 8.2.

Starting point Road Junction M 5 c 96.20.

Starting point for 1/1st E.L.Field Ambulance, Junction of SWITCH Road and DUNKERQUE - POPERINGHE Road.

3.
Order of march	Time at Starting Point.
Brigade Headquarters.	9.27.a.m.
7th Lan Fus.	9.31.a.m.
8th " "	10.3.a.m.
5th " "	10.25.a.m.
6th " "	10.39.a.m.
125th M.G.Company.	11.a.m.
125th T.M.Battery.	11.7.a.m.
427th Field Coy.R.E.	11.10.a.m.
429th Coy. A.S.C.	11.19.a.m.
1/1st E.L.Field Amb.	12.34.p.m.

4. (a). Companies will march at 300 yards interval, Battalion Headquarters will not march as a separate body.
1st Line Transport will march 300 yards in rear of the rear Company of its Unit.

(b). Machine Gun Company and 427th Field Company R.E., including 1st Line transport will march closed up.

(c). All Transport will move closed up to the regulation distance (i.e. 4 yards).

(d). Baggage Wagons will march with train.

(e). Attention is directed to XIX Corps G.709/13 of 23/6/17, paras 1 & 3.

5. Billeting Parties will meet the Staff Captain at Cross Roads L 2 a 50.75 at 9.a.m. 19th inst.

6. Units will report arrival in new areas and forward a march state within 1 Hour after arrival in Camp.

7. A watch for Synchronization will be sent round to Units to-night by Signal Officer.

8. Brigade Headquarters will close at H 7 a 2.2. at 8.30.a.m. and open at ST JAN - TER - BIEZEN at 12 Noon.

9. A C K N O W L E D G E.

Captain,
Brigade Major,
125th BRIGADE.

Issued at 1.p.m. through Signals.
Copies to:-
1. 5th Lan Fus.   10. Brigade Major.
2. 6th " "   11. Staff Captain.
3. 7th " "   12. Signal Officer.
4. 8th " "   13. B. T. O.
5. 125th M.G.Company. 14. T. M. ST JAN - TER - BIEZEN.
6. 125th T.M.Battery. 15. 42nd Division.
7. 427th Field Coy R.E. 16.) War Diary.
8. 429th Coy A.S.C.   17.)
9. 1/1st E.L.Field Amb. 18. F I L E.

SECRET.　　　　　　　　　　　　　　　　　　　　　Copy No.

125TH BRIGADE OPERATION ORDER NO. 40.

20/9/17.

1.　　As far as is known at present the 125th Brigade Group, less transport (to include 427th Field Coy. R.E. and 1/1st E.L. Field Ambulance), will proceed by rail from ST. JAN TER BIEZEN Area to the ARNEKE Area, on 22nd inst.

2.　　Transport will proceed by road on the same date.

3.　　Confirmation will be sent later.

4.　　A C K N O W L E D G E.

　　　　　　　　　　　　　　　　　　　　　Captain,
　　　　　　　　　　　　　　　　　　　　　Brigade Major,
　　　　　　　　　　　　　　　　　　　　　125th. BRIGADE.

Issued at 4. p.m.
Copies to :-

1. 5th. Lan Fus.
2. 6th.　 "　 "
3. 7th.　 "　 "
4. 8th.　 "　 "
5. 125th. M.G. Company.
6. 125th. T.M. Battery.
7. 427th Fd. Coy. R.E.
8. 429th Coy. A.S.C.
9. 1/1st. E.L. Field Amb.
10. Brigade Major.
11. Staff Captain.
12. Bde. T.O.
13. 42nd Division.
14.)
15.) War Diary.
16. F I L E.

SECRET.   Copy No. 15.

125TH BRIGADE OPERATION ORDER NO. 40.

20/9/17.

1. As far as is known at present the 125th Brigade Group, less transport (to include 427th Field Coy. R.E. and 1/1st E.L. Field Ambulance), will proceed by rail from ST. JAN TER BIEZEN Area to the ARNEKE Area, on 22nd inst.

2. Transport will proceed by road on the same date.

3. Confirmation will be sent later.

4. A C K N O W L E D G E.

                                                Captain,
                                            Brigade Major,
                                            125th. BRIGADE.

Issued at 4. p.m.
Copies to :-

1. 5th. Lan Fus.
2. 6th. "   "
3. 7th. "   "
4. 8th. "   "
5. 125th. M.G. Company.
6. 125th. T.M. Battery.
7. 427th Fd. Coy. R.E.
8. 429th Coy. A.S.C.
9. 1/1st. E.L. Field Amb.
10. Brigade Major.
11. Staff Captain.
12. Bde. T.O.
13. 42nd Division.
14.)
15.) War Diary.
16. F I L E.

SECRET.   Copy no. 16

ADDENDUM NUMBER 1 TO 125th BRIGADE O.O.No.40.   21/9/17.

1. Para 1 of Brigade Order Number 40 is confirmed.

   The Brigade Group will entrain at HOPOUTRE, L 17 d 6.8. at times to be notified later. A careful reconnaisance of the Route will be made by each Unit.

2. (a). Transport will march under orders of O.C.429th Company A.S.C. direct to ARNEKE via HERZEELE and WORMHOUDT. Head of Column to reach ARNEKE by 2p.m. Transport of each Unit to be closed up; 400 yards between Units.

   (b). 1 Limber per Unit may be left to bring on Dixies. They will march at 1p.m. under orders of a Transport Officer to be detailed by O.C. Machine Gun Company.

3. Arrival of Units including Transport to be reported to Brigade Headquarters immediately.

4. Billeting Parties from each Unit on Bicycles will meet Lieut NORTH at the Town Major's Office, ARNEKE at 9.a.m. 22nd inst. They will parade at the junction of the Camp Road and WATOU ROAD at 6.a.m., and march in a formed body under the Senior Officer present. 1/1st E.L.Field Ambulance Billeting party will proceed by Motor Ambulance.

5. The Brigade Group will move on 24th inst to the FOURTH ARMY Area and be billeted at GHYVELDE.

   The Division will take over a portion of the Front on 24th and 25th.

6. A C K N O W L E D G E.

                                            A.Lawrence
                                            Captain,
                                            Brigade Major,
                                            125th BRIGADE.

Issued at 12.Noon through Signals.

Copies to:-
1. 5th Lan Fus.   10. B.T.O.
2. 6th   "   ".   11. Brigade Major.
3. 7th   "   "   12. Staff Captain.
4. 8th   "   "   13. Signal Officer.
5. 125th M.G.Company.   14. Lieut. CLEMES.
6. 125th T.M.Battery.   15. 42nd Division.
7. 427th Field Coy R.E.   16.) War Diary.
8. 429th Coy A.S.C.   17.)
9. 1/1st E.L.Fd Amb.   18. F I L E.

SECRET. Copy No...12...

125th, BRIGADE WARNING ORDER NO. 41.

24/9/17.

MapRef: 1:20.000. COXYDE sheet, and
Sheet 19. 1:40.000.

1. 125th Brigade will move to ST. IDESBALD. tomorrow.

2. Advance parties will move about 10.a.m., Main Body about 1.p.m,
Times will be notified later.

3. 427th Field Coy.R.E. and 1/1st E.L. Field Amb, will receive
orders from C.R.E. and A.D.M.S. respectively.

4. 1 Officer and 25 O.R. from each Battalion will report to O.C.
427th. Fd.Coy.R.EM by 8.a.m. tomorrow.

They will be rationed up to 26th inst inclusive by units.

Captain,
Brigade Major,
125th. BRIGADE.

Issued at 6,p.m.

Copies to :-

1. 5th. Lan Fus.
2. 6th.   "   "
3. 7th.   "   "
4. 8th.   "   "
5. 125th.M.G.COY.
6. 125th.T.M.B.
7th 125th. Bde.T.O.
8. 427th. Fd.Coy.R.E.
9t 429th. Coy.A.S.C.
10, 1/1st E.L. Fd,Amb.
11.)
12.) War Diary.
13. F I L E.

S E C R E T.　　　　　　　　　　　　　　　　　　　　　　Copy No....

125th BRIGADE ORDER NUMBER 42.　　　　　25/9/17.

Ref Maps.　SHEETS 19 $\frac{1}{40,000}$ & FOURNES $\frac{1}{40,000}$

1. The 42nd Division less Artillery are relieving the 66th Division less Artillery in the NIEUPORT BAINS Area Sector and COXYDE BAINS Coast Defence Sector.

2. Headquarters 42nd Division will open at ST IDESBALD at 10.a.m. to-day, when G.O.C. 42nd Division will assume Command of the Sector.
   127th Brigade will hold the NIEUPORT BAINS Sector.
   126th Brigade the COXYDE BAINS SECTOR.

3. The 125th Brigade and 429th Company A.S.C. will move to-morrow and relieve the 199th Brigade in the ST IDESBALD Area as follows:-

4. Route via Main DUNKERQUE - FURNES Road - ADINKERKE - LA PANNE - Sea Shore.
   Starting Point Cross Roads D 15 b 6.6.

UNIT.	TIMES AT STARTING POINT.
Brigade Headquarters.	1.p.m.
8th Lan Fus.	1.2.p.m.
7th Lan Fus.	1.17.p.m.
5th Lan Fus.	1.32.p.m.
Machine Gun Coy.	1.42.p.m.
Trench Mortar Battery.	1.45.p.m.
6th Lan Fus.	1.47.p.m.

   Units will not enter the Camps in ST IDESBALD Area before 4.p.m., unless the outgoing Units have left.

5. Distances of 200 yards will be kept between Companies. Battalion Headquarters will move as a Company; the Machine Gun Company will move as one Company. Companies will not Halt because the Company in Front has Halted until they have closed up.

6. The transport of the Brigade and the 429th Company A.S.C. will march under orders of O.C. 429th Company A.S.C. as follows:-

7. Route Main FURNES - DUNKERQUE Road - ADINKERKE - LA PANNE - DE ZEPANNE. - KERKPANNE
   Starting Point Cross Roads D 15 b 6.6.

UNIT.	TIME AT STARTING POINT.
Brigade Headquarters	2.p.m.
8th Lan Fus.	2.2.p.m.
7th Lan Fus.	2.6.p.m.
5th Lan Fus.	2.10.p.m.
Machine Gun Company.	2.14.p.m.
6th Lan Fus.	2.18.p.m.
429th Company A.S.C.	2.22.p.m.

8. The Transport of each Unit will march in 2 Sections with 200 yards between each Section.

(2)

9. Billeting Parties from each Unit (except 429th Company A.S.C.) will rendezvous at the Church GHYVELDE at 10.a.m. and report to Lieut NORTH at Town Major's Office ST IDESBALD at 12 Noon.

10. 7th Lan Fus will find a Working Party of 3 Companies (not less than 350 all Ranks), to report to 104th Tunnelling Company R.E. at SURREY Camp R 32 b 5.6, at 10.a.m. 26th inst. They will be rationed up to the 27th inst inclusive. Cookers to accompany each Company.

11. Brigade Headquarters will close at GHYVELDE at 12 Noon and open at ST IDESBALD on arrival.

12. A Watch will be sent round to Units for Synchronisation by Brigade Signal Officer.

13. A C K N O W L E D G E.

A. Lawrence
Captain,
Brigade Major,
125th BRIGADE.

Issued at 6.a.m.

Copies to:-

1. 5th La n Fus.
2. 6th Lan Fus.
3. 7th La n Fus.
4. 8th Lan Fus.
5. 125th Machine Gun Company.
6. 125th Trench Mortar Battery.
7. 427th Field Company R.E.
8. 429th Company A.S.C.
9. Brigade Major.
10. Staff Captain.
11. Signal Officer.
12. B. T. O.
13. T. M. GHYVELDE.
14. T.M. ST IDESBALD.
15. 42nd Division.
16. 126th Brigade.
17. 127th Brigade.
18. 199th Brigade.
19.) War Diary.
20.)
21. F I L E.
22. Lieut CLEMES.

CONFIDENTIAL.

WAR DIARY of
125TH L.T. TRENCH MORTAR BATTERY.

Oct 1st - 31st. 1917

Vol VI

WAR DIARY
INTELLIGENCE SUMMARY
(Erase heading not required.)

Army Form C. 2118

125 Light T. & M. Bob. Battery

Place	Date	Hour	MAP. REF.	Summary of Events and Information	Remarks and references to Appendices
COXYDE-BAINS.	1st		COXYDE 1/20000.	HDQRS AT W.6.a.15.35.	APC
"	2nd		"	ORDERS RECEIVED TO RELIEVE 97TH L.T.M.B. IN THE LINE ON NIGHT 5-6TH	APC
NIEUPORT.	5th	2.15 P.M.	LOMBARTZYDE 1/20000	ADVANCE PARTY 1 OFF. 20 ORS. PROCEED TO NIEUPORT TOWN TO TAKE OVER HDQRS. MARCHING VIA COXYDE VILLAGE, OOST-DUNKERQUE, WULPEN, MEETING 97TH L.T.M.B. GUIDES AT S.4.a.15.25.	APC
"	"	5.15 P.M.	"	ARRIVE AT HDQRS.	APC
"	"	6.45 P.M.	"	1ST RELIEF PROCEEDS TO LINE. FORWARD HDQRS IN REDAN AT M.28.b.R.3. FOUR GUNS WERE TAKEN OVER COMPLETE IN LINE.	APC
"	"	8.50 - 10.0 P.M. - 1 A.M.	"	RELIEF TAKES PLACE. ARRANGEMENTS MADE TO PLACE 6 GUNS IN THE LINE. N°1. IN SUPPORT LINE; 2 AND 3 IN THIRD LINE CO-ORDINATES AS FOLLOWS: M.23.c.80.40. M.23.c.40.40. M.23.c.15.40. N°4. GUN AT APEX OF OUTER REDAN AT M.28.b.0.5. N°s 5 AND 6 IN PRESQU'ILE AT M.22.d.55.75.	APC
"	8th	11.0 P.M.	"	GUNS FOR PRESQU'ILE BROUGHT UP AND PLACED IN POSITION.	APC
"	9th	-	"	N° 305,391 PTE. E. HICKSON PROMOTED LANCE-CORPL.	APC
"	11th	5.30 P.M.	"	N° 305 391 L-CPL HICKSON. E. WOUNDED WHILE PROCEEDING ON LIGHT TRENCH MORTAR COURSE AT XVTH CORPS T.M. SCHOOL. ALSO N° 295016 PTE KEARNS.	APC
"	12th	11.15 A.M.	"	1 OFFICER, 1 N.C.O. PROCEED ON GAS COURSE. GUN AT M.23.c.84. FIRED 15 ROUNDS IN RETALIATION TO ENEMY T.M. FIRE.	APC
"	15th	4.0 P.M.	"	O.C. 147TH L.T.M.B. AND SECOND IN COMMAND VISIT HDQRS AT M.28.c.85.15. ALSO ADVANCED HDQRS AT M.28.b.45. N° 1 GUN FIRED AGAIN IN RETALIATION ENEMY T.M. ACTIVITY. ABOUT 40 ROUNDS FIRED.	APC
"	16th	7.30 A.M.	"	N° 241430 PTE RIGG AND N°30183 PTE LONSDALE WOUNDED WHILST CARRYING AMM. TO RIGHT POSITIONS.	APC
"	17th	8.0 P.M.	"	N°s 2 + 3 GUNS FIRED 25 ROUNDS IN RETALIATION FOR ENEMY T.M. FIRE.	APC
"	18th		LOMBARTZYDE 1/20000	PARTY RETURNS FROM GAS COURSE. 1 OFF. PROCEEDS ON LEAVE.	APC

Army Form C. 2118

/125 Light Trench Mortar Battery

WAR DIARY
INTELLIGENCE SUMMARY
(Erase heading not required.)

Instructions regarding War Diaries and Intelligence Summaries are contained in F. S. Regs., Part II. and the Staff Manual respectively. Title Pages will be prepared in manuscript.

Place	Date	Hour	MAP.REF.	Summary of Events and Information	Remarks and references to Appendices
NIEUPORT.	21ST.	7:15PM	LOMBARTZYDE. 1/20,000.	SECOND IN COMMAND 127TH L.T.M.B. GOES ROUND FORWARD POSITIONS PREVIOUS TO RELIEF.	APC.
"	22ND.	10:0PM		BATTERY RELIEVED BY 127TH L.T.M.B. ALL GUNS TAKEN OVER BY THEM LESS THE ACCESSORIES.	APC.
"	23RD.	12:30AM	"	UNABLE TO CROSS OVER FROM REDAN TO NIEUPORT AS ALL BRIDGES WERE BROKEN.	APC.
		1:15AM		CROSSED OVER PUTNEY BRIDGE.	APC.
		1:45AM		RELIEF COMPLETED; BATTERY MARCHES TO COXYDE-VILLE	APC.
		4:30AM	COXYDE 1/20,000	HDQRS ESTABLISHED IN CANADA CAMP AT W.18. L.75.35.	APC.
	24TH.	-		No. 200333 CPL. WOOD. PROCEEDS ON GAS COURSE.	APC.
	25TH.			3 O.R.S. PROCEED ON LEAVE.	APC.
	28TH.			No. 200333 CPL. WOOD RETURNS FROM GAS COURSE.	APC.
	31ST.	12NOON.		No. 29302.95 6T THOMPSON. L. PROCEEDS ON GAS COURSE.	APC.

O.C.
125TH LIGHT TRENCH MORTAR BATTERY.

1875 Wt. W593/826 1,000,000 4/15 J.B.C. & A. A.D.S.S./Forms/C. 2118.

WAR DIARY
INTELLIGENCE SUMMARY
(Erase heading not required.)

Army Form C. 2118

CONFIDENTIAL.

WAR DIARY
of
125 LIGHT TRENCH MORTAR BATTERY
Nov. 1st to 30th
1917
Vol. No. 7

WAR DIARY
or
INTELLIGENCE SUMMARY

(Erase heading not required.)

Army Form C. 2118

Place	Date	Hour	MAP.REF.	Summary of Events and Information	Remarks and references to Appendices
COXIDE CANADA CAMP	30th–7th Sept-Nov. 2nd	– 7:30 AM	COXYDE 1/10000	PERIOD RESTING IN CANADA CAMP AT W.13 b/ 16.35. N° 2950.49 SGT.THOMPSON.L. PROCEEDS ON GAS COURSE.	AFC AFC
	6th	8:45 PM	"	" RETURNS FROM COURSE.	AFC
	7th & 8th	–	N° 5 2nd ED. 1/10000	PTE. SHELMERDINE. REPORTS TO BATTERY. RELIEF TAKES PLACE ; 12.5 L.T.M.B. RELIEVE 127 L.T.M.B. IN THE LINE.	AFC
	7th	1:45 PM	"	SECOND LIEUT. L.L. DAVIES & NO. O.R'S. PROCEED TO NIEUPORT ON FIRST RELIEF ARRIVING THERE AT 4 P.M. AS SOON AS DARK 1st RELIEF TAKES PLACE. 6 GUN STAKEN OVER ON POSITIONS. HDQRS. IN NIEUPORT, AT CORNER OF RUE LONGUE CO-ORDINATES : M.28.C.85.15. ADVANCED HDQRS. AT REDAN. M.28.b.10.15. ALL GUN POSITIONS WERE AS HANDED OVER PREVIOUSLY TO 127 LTMB. EXCEPT IN THE CASE OF N°4 GUN, IN NEW EMPLACEMENT AT M.28.b. 16.35.	AFC
	10th	2:30–4 PM	"	ENEMY FIRES INTERMITTANTLY ON NIEUPORT — DIRECT HIT OBTAINED ON BATTERY HDQRS. CASUALTIES : KILLED 1 DIED OF WOUNDS 1 WOUNDED 3. C.O. SLIGHTLY WOUNDED REMAIN AT DUTY. PTE. WILKINSON. REPORTS TO BATTERY.	NATURE OF GUN 8-INCH ARMOUR-PIERCING. PTE WARD A. DIED AT 36 C.C.S. 17 MANCHESTER REGT. PTE SLATER. J. KILLED. " SLATER. W. " BARLOW. " MIDDLETON WOUNDED.
	14th	3:0 AM	"	N° 1 FIRES IN RETALIATION TO H.T.M. 6 ROUNDS WERE FIRED ON PINE HOUSE.	AFC
	15th	2:0 AM	"	" FIRED AGAIN 8 MORE ROUNDS ON LORRY TRENCH.	
	"	2:35 AM	"	N° 2 & 3 GUNS FIRED 14 ROUNDS ON LORRY TRENCH.	
	16th	1:30 AM	"	N° 7 GUN FIRED THREE ROUNDS WITH ALLWAYS FUSE.	
	17th	4:0 AM	"	N° 1 FIRED 8 ROUNDS ON LORRY TRENCH, 8 ROUNDS ON PINE HOUSE.	AFC
COXYDE	19th	8:30 PM	COXYDE 1/10000	BATTERY LEAVE THE LINE. NO UNIT RELIEVED, AS THEY ARE N°2 BRIGADE T.M. BATTERIES WITH THE FRENCH. PULL OUT AFTER DARK, AND SPEND NIGHT AT AUSTRALIA CAMP.	AFC
	20th	7:15 AM	"	MARCH TO ADINKERQUE VIA LA PANNE. CROSS ROAD & THENCE BY BARGE TO BERGUES VIA HAZE BROUCK & VIA DUNKERQUE, ARRIVING BERGUES AT 3:30 P.M. THENCE BY MARCH ROUTE TO WORMHOUT, ARRIVING THERE AT 6:30 P.M.	AFC

WAR DIARY
INTELLIGENCE SUMMARY
(Erase heading not required.)

Army Form C. 2118

Instructions regarding War Diaries and Intelligence Summaries are contained in F.S. Regs., Part II. and the Staff Manual respectively. Title Pages will be prepared in manuscript.

Place	Date	Hour	MAP.REF.	Summary of Events and Information	Remarks and references to Appendices
WORMHOUDT	21st	8.30 AM	HAZEBROUK. 1/40000	MOVE FROM WORMHOUT TO L'ANGE BY MARCH ROUTE ARRIVING THERE AT 12 NOON.	NEAR CASSEL. A.W.
	22nd	8.15 AM	"	" " FARM NEAR OXELAERE " 1.20 P.M.	A.W.
	23rd	8.50 AM	"	BATTERY MOVE BY MARCH ROUTE TO PECQUEUR ARRIVING THERE AT 12.40 P.M.	A.W.
	27th	7.30 AM	"	STAY AT PECQUEUR THREE DAYS. BATTERY MOVE BY MARCH ROUTE TO BÉTHUNE. VIA : ST VENANT + ROBECQ.	SECOND IN COMMAND, PROCEEDS BY MOTOR LORRY DIRECT TO LINE.
	28th	6.45 AM	BÉTHUNE 1/40000	" LE PRÉOL ARRIVING THERE AT 8.0 AM.	A.W.
	"	8.15 AM	LABASSÉE 1/10000	BATTERY MOVE INTO LINE AND RELIEVE 75th L.T.M.B. HDQRS ESTABLISHED AT F.10.d.60.25. 6 GUNS PLACED IN POSITION, 3 GUNS ON RIGHT BATTALION FRONT, 3 GUNS ON LEFT BATT. FRONT. CO-ORDINATES FOR EMPLACEMENTS: 1. A 27.b.30.85. 4. A 21.b.75.15. 2. A 21.d.60.55. 5. A 15.d.35.05. 3. A 21.b.36.45. 6. A 15.b.65.70.	No 3 NOT YET PLACED IN POSITION. A.W.
	28th	12.15 PM	"	3 ROUNDS FIRED ON BRICKBAT ALLEY. FROM No 4. RETALIATION.	A.W.
	"	1.15 PM	"	3 ROUNDS " " FRANK'S KEEP.	
	29th	10.15 PM	"	20 ROUNDS FIRED FROM No 4 ON BRICKBAT ALLEY + VICINITY. SEVERAL ROUNDS FIRED BY No 1 + No 2 ON FRANK'S KEEP.	A.W.
	30th	—	"	70 ROUNDS FIRED IN COURSE OF DAY ON BRICKBAT, SPOTTED DOG ALLEY. FROM No 4 GUN.	A.W.
	30th	7.15 PM	"	ENEMY ATTEMPTS RAID ON SECTOR ON OUR RIGHT OCCUPIED BY PORTUGUESE TROOPS.	A.W.

O.C.
125th L.T.M. BATTERY.

WAR DIARY
INTELLIGENCE SUMMARY
(Erase heading not required.)

Army Form C. 2118

Summary of Events and Information

of

125 Light Trench Mortar Battery

From 1 Dec. 1917 to 31st Dec. 1917

CONFIDENTIAL

Army Form C. 2118

WAR DIARY
INTELLIGENCE SUMMARY
(Erase heading not required.)

Instructions regarding War Diaries and Intelligence Summaries are contained in F. S. Regs., Part II. and the Staff Manual respectively. Title Pages will be prepared in manuscript.

Place	Date	Hour	Summary of Events and Information	Remarks and references to Appendices
			MAP REF.	
LE PRÉOL	1.12.17	10.30 AM	LABASSÉE 1/10000. BATTERY TOOK OVER FROM 176TH L.T.M.B. ON RIGHT SECTOR. SIX GUNS WERE PUT IN THE LINE. CO-ORDINATES AS FOLLOWS: Nº 1. A.21.d.50.05. 2. A.21.d.55.55. 3. A.21.d.50.85. 4. A.21.b.75.75. 5. A.21.b.76.78. 6. A.15.b.65.65. 7 IN RESERVE. SEC. HDQRS. WERE ESTABLISHED AT. A.21.c.80.65.	A.P.C.
"			"	
"			BÉTHUNE 1/40000 HDQRS WERE ESTABLISHED AT F.10.c.8.2.	
IN THE LINE.	4.12.17.	10 P.M.	A PREMATURE EXPLOSION OCCURRED ON Nº 2 GUN; KILLING PTES. TOOTAL & KIRK.	A.P.C.
	8.12.17	8.30 AM	LABASSÉE 1/10000. L-CORPL. DEAN, & MITCHELL PROCEED ON T.M. COURSE AT XV CORPS SCHOOL.	A.P.C.
BÉTHUNE	10.12.17		BÉTHUNE 1/40000 BATTERY RELIEVED IN THE LINE BY 176TH L.T.M.B. & MARCHED TO BÉTHUNE.	A.P.C.
	13.12.17.	8.30 AM.	L-CORPL. SEAL PROCEEDS ON GAS COURSE. DIV. GAS COURSE.	A.P.C.
	20.12.17.	P.M.	BATTERY CHRISTMAS DINNER.	A.P.C.
	22.12.17.	8.30 AM	BÉTHUNE AND LABASSÉE MARCH TO GORRE AND TAKE OVER ON LEFT SECTOR OF DIVISIONAL FRONT FROM 127 L.T.M.BTY. AT FESTUBERT. 7 GUNS WERE PUT IN THE LINE COORDINATES AS FOLLOWS: 1. A.9.d.22.07. 3. A.9.a.10.75. 4. A.9.a.90.07. 5. A.9.a.85.09. 6. A.3.a.65.65. 7. A.3.a.75.62.	
BÉTHUNE			BATTERY HDQRS WERE ESTABLISHED AT FESTUBERT AT X.3.d.6.5.	A.P.C.

Army Form C. 2118

WAR DIARY
INTELLIGENCE SUMMARY
(Erase heading not required.)

Instructions regarding War Diaries and Intelligence Summaries are contained in F. S. Regs., Part II. and the Staff Manual respectively. Title Pages will be prepared in manuscript.

Place	Date	Hour	MAP REF.	Summary of Events and Information	Remarks and references to Appendices
IN THE LINE	22.12.17	11-0 NOON	LABASSEE 1/10000 AND BETHUNE 1/40000	SEC. HDQRS WERE ESTABLISHED AT S.26.a.75.85: AND. A.9.c.10.75.	A.C.
	24.12.17	7.30 PM	LABASSEE 1/10000	A SPECIAL SHOOT WAS CARRIED OUT, IN CONJUNCTION WITH PROJECTION OF GAS ON H. LINES SOME 240 ROUNDS BARRAGING FIRE WERE FIRED ON HIS FRONT LINE. NO CASUALTIES OCCURRED.	A.P.C.
	28.12.17	8.0 AM.	BETHUNE 1/40000	PTE ARMSTRONG PROCEEDED ON COURSE AT BDE. SIGNALS.	A.C.
	29.12.17	8.30 AM	—	2 LIEUT. DAVIES. L.L. PROCEEDED ON GENERAL COURSE OF INSTRUCTION AT 1ST ARMY INFANTRY SCHOOL.	

SIGND A.P.Morgan Lieut.
FOR.
O.C. COMMANDING
125TH LIGHT T.M. BTY.

Army Form C. 2118

WAR DIARY
or
INTELLIGENCE SUMMARY
(Erase heading not required.)

OF

125 Light Trench Mortar Battery

From 1st Jan 1918 to 31st Jan 1918.

CONFIDENTIAL

Ref. Map BETHUNE
Sheet 1 — 1/40,000

WAR DIARY
or
INTELLIGENCE SUMMARY
(Erase heading not required.)

Army Form C. 2118

Place	Date	Hour	Summary of Events and Information	Remarks and references to Appendices
FESTUBERT S.25.d.5.4	14/4/18		2nd Lieut. J.V. Jacoby 1/5 Lanc. Fus. attached to Battery for duty.	
GIVENCHY A9c9.1	5/4/18		5 O.R. killed by enemy T.M. shell dropping on No 4 Position, and exploding ammunition.	
FAUQUIS ROT A21.d.8.8	16/4/18		2 O.R. proceeded on T.M. Instructors Course at 1st Corps School, duration 2 weeks.	
LOCON	17/4/18		1 O.R. proceeded on 8 week course at Divl. Signalling School.	
PROSPER SP ROT A21.d.8.8	17/4/18		2 N.C.O.s proceeded on 3 days Course on Allways Fuse 1st Corps School.	
FESTUBERT S.25.d.5.4	19/4/18 1.0 P.M.		Battery relieved by 126 L.T.M.By and moved by march route to rest billet in BEUVRY. H.Q. of F14.d.7.0	
BEUVRY F14.d.7.0	28/4/18 4.P.M.		Advance party of 3 N.C.O.s proceeded to Canal Sector from to relieve 129 L.T.M.By.	
—do—	29/4/18 9.A.M.		Battery moved by march route to Le Preol, and relieved 129 L.T.M.By in the Canal Sector. Guns taken over in position.	

N.V. Dickson
Capt.
O.C. 125 L.T.M.By

Army Form C. 2118

WAR DIARY
INTELLIGENCE SUMMARY
(Erase heading not required.)

Summary of Events and Information

OF

125 Light Trench Mortar Battery

FROM
1st February 1918
TO
28th February 1918.

CONFIDENTIAL.

WAR DIARY or INTELLIGENCE SUMMARY

Army Form C. 2118

Place	Date	Hour	Summary of Events and Information	Remarks and references to Appendices
LE PREUX F10 d 5,5	1/2/18 3/2/18		Battery in line CANAL SECTOR. 2nd Lieut L.L. DAVIES returned off General Course of Instruction at 1st Army School.	
	9/2/18	2-0 P.M.	1 O.R. killed in action by enemy T.M. Shell.	
	10/—	11-0 A.M.	Lieut A.P. COOPER posted and proceeded to join 21st Batt. MIDDLESEX REGT.	
	15/—		Lieut. P. STRUB, Intelligencer attached to the Battery	
	—	3-30 P.M.	Battery relieved in CANAL SECTOR by 164 L.T.M. BY, and moved by route march to DROUVIN.	
DROUVIN K 4 c 5,7	21/2/18		1 O.R. proceeded on Course at 1st Corps Gun School.	
	24/—		2nd Lieut F.V. JACOBY & 2 O.R's proceeded on Course at 1st Corps T.M. School.	

J.K. Benson
Capt.
O.C. 125 L.T.M. BY

42nd Division

125th Infantry Brigade

125th LIGHT TRENCH MORTAR BATTERY

MARCH 1 9 1 8

WAR DIARY
INTELLIGENCE SUMMARY.
(Erase heading not required.)

Army Form C. 2118

125 LIGHT TRENCH MORTAR BATTERY

from
1st MARCH 1918.
to
31st MARCH 1918

VOL. 14

CONFIDENTIAL

WAR DIARY / INTELLIGENCE SUMMARY

Army Form C. 2118

Place	Date	Hour	Summary of Events and Information	Remarks and references to Appendices
DROUVIN K.14.c.5.7 (Bethune Coal Field)	1/3/18		Battery in G.H.Q. Reserve.	
—do—	11/3/18		Capt A Dickson proceeded on leave to U.K. Lieut G. OSBOURN assumed command of the Battery.	
—do—	23/—/—	2.0 AM	Battery ordered to Embus for Strategical move.	
ADINFER WOOD F.2.c.9.9 (Sheet 57d.) (1/40,000)	—do—	1.0 PM	Battery arrived at ADINFER WOOD and bivouacced.	
—do—	24/—/—	5.0 PM	Battery moved by march route to COURCELCOURT to relieve 120 L.T.M. By.	
COURCELCOURT (Sheet 57d.SH) F.30.c.7.3 (Sheet 57d 1/40,000)	—do—	11.0 PM	Battery returned by march route to LOB EAST WOOD	
LOB EAST WOOD 25/3/18		5.0 PM	Battery withdrawn by march route to ADINFER WOOD.	
ADINFER WOOD F.2.c.9.9	26/—/—	1.0 PM	Battery moved by march route to BIENVILLIERS at Btn Transport Lines	
BIENVILLIER 27/—/— E.10.5.5 (Sheet 57d 1/40,000)		5.0 PM	Battery moved into the line (H.Q. at ESSARTS) employed in carrying Bombs.	
ESSARTS 75 E.30.1.2	30/4/—/—	1.0 AM	Battery moved into Close at COURCELCOURT. (H.Q. at E.29.a.8.4 Sheet 57d 1/40,000)	

N N Drew
Capt.
O.C. 125 L.T.M.By

125th Inf.Bde.
42nd Div.

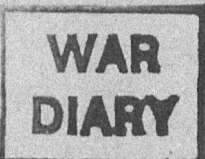

125th LIGHT TRENCH MORTAR BATTERY.

A P R I L

1 9 1 8

Army Form C. 2118

WAR DIARY
or
INTELLIGENCE SUMMARY

(Erase heading not required.)

Instructions regarding War Diaries and Intelligence Summaries are contained in F. S. Regs., Part II. and the Staff Manual respectively. Title Pages will be prepared in manuscript.

Volume No. 18.

125 Light Trench Mortar Battery.

From 1st April 1918.
to 30th April 1918.

CONFIDENTIAL.

Place	Date	Hour	Summary of Events and Information	Remarks and references to Appendices

INTELLIGENCE SUMMARY

(Erase heading not required.)

Instructions regarding War Diaries and Intelligence Summaries are contained in F. S. Regs., Part II. and the Staff Manual respectively. Title Pages will be prepared in manuscript.

Place	Date	Hour	Summary of Events and Information	Remarks and references to Appendices
COMMECOURT ESSARTS do.	1/4/18 4/—		Battery in Reserve with H.Q. at E.29 a.8.4. Sheet 57.D 1/40.000 Capt. A.A. DICKSON returned from leave to U.K. and Later over command of the Battery.	
do.	5/4/18		Germans attacked BUCQUOY, 2 Guns destroyed by shell fire, 5 O.R°. wounded and 4 gassed. Lieut. J.W. WILKINSON returned from Leave at 1st Corps. T.M. School. Heavy bombardment by gas shells around H.Q. at ESSARTS.	
	6/—	12 O.R°. gassed.	
	8/4/18	5·0 AM	Battery relieved by 185th T.M.B. and moved by bus to VAUCHELLES, H.Q. at 133.c. Sheet 57.D 1/40,000	
VAUCHELLES	13/4/18 133.c.	4·30 AM	Battery moved by march route and bivouaced in WARNIMONT WOOD. Capt. A.A. DICKSON wounded, Lieut. G. OSBOURN takes over command.	
	15/—			
WARNIMONT WOOD	17/4/18	3·07 PM	Battery moved by march route to CONNECOURT and relieved 112 T.M.B. in the Line. H.Q. at K.4 d.30.35. Sheet 57.D. N.E. Capt. A.A. DICKSON transferred to England.	
	20/4/18			
CONNECOURT K.4 d. 30.35	29/4/18	1·25 AM	Battery relieved in Line by 129 T.M.B., and moved into Divist Reserve at BAYENCOURT.	

G. Osbourn Lieut
O.C. 125. L.T.M.B.Y

Army Form C. 2118.

WAR DIARY
INTELLIGENCE SUMMARY.
(Erase heading not required.)

Summary of Events and Information

of

125 Light Trench Mortar Battery

from 1st May 1918.
to 31st May 1918.

CONFIDENTIAL.

Place	Date	Hour	Summary of Events and Information	Remarks and references to Appendices

125TH TRENCH MORTAR BATTERY.
No. E44
Date 2/6/18

To
125 Bde.

Ref. A.L. 183 of 2/6/18.

Volume No. for War Diary —
May 1918 :— No. 16.

J Osborn Capt
O.C.
125 L.T.M.By

Army Form C. 2118.

WAR DIARY
INTELLIGENCE SUMMARY.
(Erase heading not required.)

Instructions regarding War Diaries and Intelligence Summaries are contained in F. S. Regs., Part II. and the Staff Manual respectively. Title pages will be prepared in manuscript.

Place	Date	Hour	Summary of Events and Information	Remarks and references to Appendices
BAYENCOURT T.10.d.40.99. Sheet 57D.N.E	1/5/18		Battery in Divisional Reserve.	
—do—		7/--	Battery moved by march route to CORNECOURT (H.Q's at E.28.d central) and relieved 126 T.M.B. in the line.	
CORNECOURT E.28.d central	6/--	3/--	1 O.R wounded. Battery relieved in the line by 171 T.M.B. and moved by march route into Army Reserve at COUIN WOODS. H.Q's at J.2.c.	
COUIN WOODS J.2.c (Sheet 57D N.E)	29/5/18		2nd Lieut. J.W. WILKINSON 8 Lane Fus. struck off strength of his Batt. and taken on establishment of the Battery.	

J O'Connor Capt.
O.C. 125. L.T.M.By

Army Form C. 2118.

WAR DIARY
INTELLIGENCE SUMMARY.
(Erase heading not required.)

125 Light Trench Mortar Battery.

from 1st June 1918
to 30th June 1918

Volume No. 14

CONFIDENTIAL.

Army Form C. 2118.

WAR DIARY
INTELLIGENCE SUMMARY.
(Erase heading not required.)

Instructions regarding War Diaries and Intelligence Summaries are contained in F. S. Regs. Part II. and the Staff Manual respectively. Title pages will be prepared in manuscript.

Place	Date	Hour	Summary of Events and Information	Remarks and references to Appendices
COUIN WOODS J.2.C. (Sheet 57D 1/40.000)	11/6/18.		Battery in Army Reserve.	
do.	12/---		Battery moved by march route to St LEGER LES AUTHIE and Divisional Reserve. (H.Q⁰ at T.12.C.6.6) relieving 111 T.M.B.	
St LEGER LES AUTHIE T.12.C.6.6	13/---		Battery moved by march route to BUS WOODS. H.Q⁰ at J.20.C.9.7.	
BUS WOODS J.20.C.9.7.	14/---		Battery moved by march route to HÉBUTERNE and relieved 127 T.M.B. in the line. H.Q⁰ at K.9.C.2.7.	
-do-	--		LIEUT L.L. DAVIES proceeded on a T.M Course at G.H.Q. Lewis Gun & Light Mortar School.	
HEBUTERNE	29/		Battery in the line.	

B Oatman
Capt⁵
O.C. 125 L.T.M.B⁺

Army Form C. 2118.

WAR DIARY

INTELLIGENCE SUMMARY.

(Erase heading not required.)

125 Light Trench Mortar
Battery

from 1st July 1918
to 31st July 1918.

Volume No. 18

CONFIDENTIAL.

Ref. Mjk. 57D. N40000

WAR DIARY
or
INTELLIGENCE SUMMARY.
(Erase heading not required.)

Army Form C. 2118.

Place	Date	Hour	Summary of Events and Information	Remarks and references to Appendices
HEBUTERNE K.9.c.2.7	1/7/18		Battery in the line.	
do.	2/—		Relieved by 3rd N.Z.L.T.M.By and moved by march route into Divisl Reserve at Bus Woods. T.20.c.9.7	
BUS WOODS T.20.c.9.7	3/—		Lieut. L.L. Davies return from course at G.H.Q. Lewis Gun and Light Mortar School.	
do.	10/—		Battery moved by march route and relieved 127 L.T.M.By in line H.Q. at K.32.a.35.10	
GOMMECOURT	26/7/18		Battery relieved by 126 L.T.M.By and moved by march route Divisional Reserve, Bus Woods T.20.c.9.7.	
BUS WOODS T.20.c.9.7	31/—		Battery in Divisional Reserve.	

J.A. Gainth
for O.C.
125 L.T.M.By.

Army Form C. 2118.

WAR DIARY
— or —
INTELLIGENCE SUMMARY.
(Erase heading not required.)

125 Light Trench Mortar Battery.

From 1st August 1918
To 31st August 1918

Volume No. 19

CONFIDENTIAL.

Ref. Maps. Sheet 57 e. & D.
1/40,000

Army Form C. 2118.

WAR DIARY
INTELLIGENCE SUMMARY.
(Erase heading not required.)

Place	Date	Hour	Summary of Events and Information	Remarks and references to Appendices
BUS WOODS (J20 c.9-7)	1/8/18		Batty. in Divisional Reserve.	
do.	3/-		Battery relieved 127 L.T.M.By in line: H.Qs. J24 d.68	
COLINCAMPS. (J24 d6-8)	15/8/16		4 Guns taken forward to SERRE with infantry	
	2/-		2 Sections (4 guns) took part in infantry attack on BEAUREGARD	
	24/-		Battery relieved in line by 126 L.T.M.By and moved out. Reserve at K.19.c.	
	23/-	8.0AM	Battery moved to SERRE. H.Q. K.36 a 8.8	
	29/-	5.0PM	Battery moved to MIRAUMONT. H.Qs. L.35.d.	
	27/-		Battery moved to PYS. H.Qs. N.2.d.2.5	
	31/-		Battery relieved 126 L.T.M.By H.Qs. at	

Norman Capt.
O.C. 7/125 L.T.M.By.

Army Form C. 2118.

WAR DIARY

~~INTELLIGENCE SUMMARY.~~

(Erase heading not required.)

125 Light Trench Mortar Battery.

From 1st Sept. 1918
to 30th Sept. 1918

Volume No. 20.

CONFIDENTIAL.

Army Form C. 2118.

WAR DIARY

~~INTELLIGENCE SUMMARY.~~

(Erase heading not required.)

Instructions regarding War Diaries and Intelligence Summaries are contained in F.S. Regs., Part II. and the Staff Manual respectively. Title pages will be prepared in manuscript.

Place	Date	Hour	Summary of Events and Information	Remarks and references to Appendices
LA BARQUE	1/9/18		Battery in Divisional Reserve.	
	3/...		Passed through 127 Bde. into line. H.Q^s BARASTRE O16 a 0.8.	
BARASTRE	5/...		Battery relieved in line, and moved by lorries to PYS. (M2d.)	
PYS.	22/9/18		Moved by march route to LEBUCQUIERE area H.Q^s at I 29 L 2.3	
	26/...		Moved into line, passing through 126 Bde. H.Q^s at Q10 d 6.8.	
	27/...		Battery co-operated in active operations. Casualties sustained Killed 2 O.R^s. Wounded 5 O.R^s.	
	29/...		NEW ZEALAND Bde. passed through 125 Bde. Battery withdrawn to H.Q^s at Q10 d 6.8	
	29/...		Battery moved into Reserve at HAVRINCOURT Wood. H.Q^s at Q8 d 20.75	

L.E. Levie
Lieut.
O.C. 125 L.T.M.By

WAR DIARY.
of
196. L.T.M.B₁.
from 1/10/18
to 31/10/18
Volume No 21
Confidential.

1st L.T.M.By
Vol 21

WAR DIARY
or
INTELLIGENCE SUMMARY.
(Erase heading not required.)

Army Form C. 2118.

Place	Date	Hour	Summary of Events and Information	Remarks and references to Appendices
HAVRINCOURT WOOD	4/10/18		Battery in Corps Reserve H.Q's at Q.F.a.20.75.	
	5/10/18		Moved by march route to VILLERS PLOUICH H.Q's R.13.b.05.40	
	9/10/18		Moved to ESNES. H.Q. at Q.4.b.4.7.	
	10/10/18		Moved to FONTAINE-AU-PIRE H.Q. I.15.c.8.3	
	11/10/18		Moved by march route to AULICOURT FARM H.Q.	
	14/10/18		Battery relieved 1 N.Z.L.T.M.By. H.Q. J.2.d.2.2	
	18/10/18		Relieved by 128 T.M.By. (with exception of Section left in line) and moved to Gonnelieu. H.Q's at I.10.a.5.8. Section took part in offensive march route to AULICOURT FARM	
	19/10/18		Relieved by 3rd N.Z.L.T.M.By. and moved by march route to BEAUVOIS. H.Q's on Farm	
	23/10/18		Relieved the 127 L.T.M.By. Moved to BRIASTRE H.Q's D.24.c.2.6	
	24/10/18		Bty. took part in offensive operations. 03:20 hours 6 guns firing March to VIESLY H.Q at D.28.d.0.9	
	29/10/18		Moved by march route to FONTAINE J.15.d.0.9	
FONTAINE	31/10/18		Battery in Corps Reserve H.Q's at J.15.d.0.9	

J.F.Davis O.C.
O.C. 125 L.T.M.By.

WAR DIARY
OF
125. L.T.M.By.
FROM 1/11/18
TO 30/11/18
VOLUME NO. 22

CONFIDENTIAL

Army Form C. 2118.

WAR DIARY
or
INTELLIGENCE SUMMARY.
(Erase heading not required.)

Instructions regarding War Diaries and Intelligence Summaries are contained in F. S. Regs., Part II. and the Staff Manual respectively. Title pages will be prepared in manuscript.

Place	Date	Hour	Summary of Events and Information	Remarks and references to Appendices
FONTAINE AU PIRE.	3/11/18		Battery in Corps Reserve HQ^s J.15. a.0.9	
	4/11/18		Moved by March Route to SOLESMES H.Q^s E.2. c.6.3 with one from 126 L.T.M.By.	
	5/11/18		Moved by March Route to BEAUDIGNIES HQ^s R.33. c.4.9.	
	6/11/18		Moved by March Route to HERBIGNIES HQ^s M.29.2-3 (Sheet 51)	
	7/—		Moved to LAHAUTE RUE. 133.a.4.1	
	8/—		Moved to BOUSSIERES HQ^s P.32.a.7.5. Battery took part in offensive operations 3 guns in the line	
	9/—		Moved to HAUTMONT HQ^s P.29.c.7.4.	
	10/—		HQ^s P.29. a.5..6	
HAUTMONT	30/11/18		Moved to	

J. Browning?
f.O.C. 125. L.T.M.By

WAR DIARY
of
125 L.T.M. By
from 1/12/18
to
31/12/18

VOLUME No. 23.

CONFIDENTIAL

Army Form C. 2118.

WAR DIARY
or
INTELLIGENCE SUMMARY.
(Erase heading not required.)

Instructions regarding War Diaries and Intelligence Summaries are contained in F. S. Regs., Part II. and the Staff Manual respectively. Title pages will be prepared in manuscript.

Place	Date	Hour	Summary of Events and Information	Remarks and references to Appendices
HAUTMONT Sheet 57	30/11/18		Battery H.Q.s P 29. a. 5. 6	
	14/12/18		Moved by March Route to MAUBEUGE	
	15/12/18		" by March Route to ESTINNE AU MONT.	
	14/12/18		" by March Route to ANDERLUES	
	18/12/18		" by March Route to CHARLEROI H.Q.s RUE DE L'ATHÉNÉE	
CHARLEROI	31/12/18		1	

J.H. Davis Lt.
O.R. 115 S.T.T.M.

www.ingramcontent.com/pod-product-compliance
Lightning Source LLC
Chambersburg PA
CBHW081241170426
43191CB00034B/1998